The Journey of a Catholic

Madukkakal

authorHOUSE®

AuthorHouse™
1663 Liberty Drive
Bloomington, IN 47403
www.authorhouse.com
Phone: 1 (800) 839-8640

Published by AuthorHouse 05/31/2018

ISBN: 978-1-5462-4072-3 (sc)
ISBN: 978-1-5462-4071-6 (e)

Library of Congress Control Number: 2018906021

Print information available on the last page.

CONTENTS

CHAPTER 1

The Conversation

I was born in a good Syro Malabar Catholic family, with loving and caring parents and a younger brother. I was blessed in every way. My brother and I had a good convent education in a reputable Jesuit school and lived our lives as normal Catholics, attending church every Sunday, going to Sunday school, and getting involved in church activities.

When I was growing up as a young adult, I started to question a lot of things, especially about God and church. I thought God was really far away or he didn't exist at all. I believed he was never involved in my life or even a part of it. At least I thought God might be somewhere out there, a force or maybe the cause of the big bang .

I never knew Jesus or believed in him, as a person or as God, a father figure who loved me and cared for me, as it says in the Bible. This made me to stop going to church or praying to Him. From my late teens to early adulthood, my life was surrounded with friends, booze, and parties. This went on until I was twenty-three.

One day, when I was home with my parents, they wanted me to drive them to a convent of nuns nearby. By this time, I had never cared to see or speak with priests or nuns. Actually, I had started to hate them. When my parents insisted that I go with them, I said, "I will go with you on one condition: I will stay in the car and you guys can go and meet this nun and come back." They agreed and went to see the nun.

While I was waiting in the car, I was pressing my shoulders because I had a very bad shoulder ache and I was on medication. When my parents came out of the convent, this particular nun followed them to the car and she saw me. They introduced this nun to me. I just looked at her and nodded, as if it didn't bother me. But to my surprise, she wanted to talk to me personally. I was surprised, as I had thought nuns didn't talk much.

I stepped out of the car and suddenly she said she wanted to talk to me alone! Now I was really puzzled and told my parents that I don't want to go in with her. But they insisted, and after much hesitation I went in with her. When we entered the room, she immediately started to pray for me. For the first time in my life, I heard these strange sounds coming out of her mouth, like birds chipping. It was not a regular prayer as I expected. I felt like laughing, but I just kept quiet and thought what in the world this old nun (she was not that old) was muttering. To my shock, she started to say all the terrible things I had been doing in my life until now. A chill went up my spine, and I started to sweat sitting there. I could not raise my eyes and look at her. Tears started to roll out of my eyes. I felt like I was being skinned and exposed to the entire world.

She said, "You need to repent of your sins. Jesus is present right here, and he is healing your shoulder."

For the first time, I felt the presence of God and his healing power. I couldn't believe myself. I moved my arms around, and the pain was gone. I came out as if nothing had happened. I didn't look at my parents, just got in the car and drove home. They thought I was upset at them about the whole ordeal and just kept quiet. Even after coming back home, I was confused about the whole thing. I said to myself, "Am I dreaming, or is it true that I have been healed? Amazing!"

As the scripture says, "I am the God who heals thee."

"Praise be to God for nuns."

A deep thirst came into my heart for God. I thought, if Jesus is real and he came to me and touched me and healed me when this nun prayed for me, I want to know this Jesus more and to know him personally.

So, on September 1998, I went for a Charismatic Renewal retreat at a retreat center. When I reached there, I was amazed at the number of people attending the retreat. The week I went, there were around 40,000 people attending the retreat, in different languages including Malayalam,

English, Hindi, Tamil, etc. I chose to go for Malayalam retreat (which was my mother tongue).

At the time, there were two huge buildings opposite each other across the main road, one for Malayalam and the other one for English and other languages.

I reached there on a Sunday afternoon. The retreat started weekly, on Sunday mornings. People were lining up for lunch after the morning secession. I was happy that it was lunchtime, as I was hungry. But there was a huge lineup for lunch, and when I looked around, I saw sick people, poor people, people in their wheel chairs, and crippled people. I was thinking, even though I lived in India, never had I seen so many poor and sick people together. When I realized that I was standing in line with these people for food, I felt that I was too good to be around these people, and I remembered that I had never stood in line for my food; it always came to the table, and my hunger left me.

I wanted to get out of this place, so I gave the steel plate back and got out of the line for food and went to my dorm and got my backpack. I started walking towards the main gate, which was facing the main road. There were security guards at the gate. When I started walking past them, one of the guards said to me in Malayalam, "You can't leave now. The gates are locked and retreat has already begun."

When I heard this, I got mad at the guard, but I didn't show it outside. Instead, I pretended that I didn't know Malayalam and started to speak to them in English. I said, "I came to the wrong building. I was supposed to go to the other side of the road, to the other building, where the English retreat is being held." They allowed me to go outside to the other building.

When I arrived outside, I was very happy. I felt like I had gotten out of prison. I started walking towards the bus, which was parked few yards from the building. On my way to the bus, there were roughly ten to fifteen beggars sitting on either side of street. They asked me, "Where are you going?"

I said, "To the English retreat center." I thought, *Why are these bums asking me this question, instead of asking for money?*

When I continued walking towards the bus, the beggars started shouting at me, "You are going in the opposite direction. The building is right behind you. I was startled at this and started to shush them. I looked around and everyone on the street and in the shops were staring at me. Hearing this noise, the security guards came running outside and asked me what had happened. Everyone looked at me as if I had stolen money from these beggars. I said to the guards, "Nothing happened. These people were just giving me the directions," and I walked towards the English retreat center.

"Thanks to the beggars on the street who led me to the Lord."

At the retreat center, the weekly retreat started on Sunday morning, with the holy Qurbana (Mass) and ended Friday afternoon. During the retreat, on Monday and Tuesday, they preached about the sins and the sacrament of repentance. During this time, you had the opportunity to go for confession and counseling. When I heard the Gospel message, I really felt sorry for my sins, and I knew what a horrible sinner I was. I repented and went for confession. I thought, "I can't remember when I went for confession last, but thank God, what a great sacrament." When I came out of the confessional, I felt as if the burdens were off my shoulders and I was cleansed.

But during these sessions, I was looking around to see if anyone was getting healed, like people getting out of wheelchairs, the blind seeing, or the lame walking, because my parents said these things are happening here. To my disappointment, over the three days, I didn't see any miracles.

On Tuesday night, I suddenly got a high fever and felt very sick. There was a doctor next to my room, who had also come to attend the retreat. He checked me and wrote a prescription, which I got from a pharmacy in the building. He said, "If the fever doesn't go down, you have to go to the hospital." This doctor was a cardiologist who had come to this retreat to be healed of his heart condition.

By Wednesday morning, the fever hadn't gone down; it stayed the same. Everyone told me to go to the hospital. Even the doctor who examined me said the same thing. I said to myself, *I came here to see others healed, and now I have a fever and am very sick. If Jesus is still the healer, as the Bible says, and if he hears my prayer, let him heal me, and I will give my entire life to him.*

I told the doctor to pray for my healing and I would pray for his. He agreed!

Wednesday was a special day to pray for physical healing. With my fever, I went and sat in the retreat hall, shivering. I was very sick and was not paying any attention to what was happening on stage. The priest was preaching on the stage. I heard him say only these words: "When Jesus passes by, he will touch you and heal you." At that moment, my faith increased, and in my heart, I knew that I would be healed. So I literally waited for Jesus to come by, like the blind Bartimaeus in the Bible.

I waited anxiously for the prayer of physical healing. During this time, everyone stood up and started to praise Jesus lifting their hands up. I also saw people clapping their hands. I had never seen anything like this in my life. Prayers at our churches were quiet and read from a book, or even in Holy Mass, never seen anyone raising their hands to praise God.

But that didn't bother me anymore. I also lifted my hands and started praising and calling on Jesus to come and touch me and heal me with my eyes shut. In few seconds, I saw someone walking near me and felt as if a cool breeze was touching me. I thought the priest was walking near me. I opened my eyes to see who was walking near me and to see where the breeze was coming from. I realized that there was no wind or breeze blowing; neither was there a fan near me. Once again, I closed my eyes, and suddenly I saw Jesus walking by. He looked at me and smiled. That very second, I started to sweat, and my fever was gone, and I was instantly healed. I started to jump up and down with amazement. I said, "Jesus, you are real. I am going to follow you all the days of my life."

I went back to the doctor who treated me, and I hugged him. "I got healed. Jesus healed me," I said.

He was happy for me and said, "My heartbeat is normal and I feel better. I thanked the Lord, and we started to praise God."

On Thursday, it was the session for inner healing. The priest said we must invite the Holy Spirit into our heart. He said he was going to pray for the past wounds that hurt the mind (subconscious) and our spirit. I didn't know what that mean at the time, so I didn't know what to expect. I heard someone say, "This is the time when the Holy Spirit comes into you." I didn't understand what the Holy Spirit did or who he was. I heard the priest say, "He is the power and mind of God. He is the third person in the Trinity.

Then I said to myself, *I want that power. I want to know God more and love him more and do his will.*

So, on Wednesday night, I earnestly started to pray for the Holy Spirit to come into my heart. Thursday was a day of fasting and prayer. For the first time in my life, I abstained from lunch. Now I realized what it is to be hungry.

At one point during the inner healing session, there was the adoration of the Blessed Sacrament. This was after the Holy Mass. At that time, we all stood up and started praising God with our hands lifted up. By now I was not ashamed to lift my hands and praise Jesus. Then the priest lifted the monstrance (where the holy Eucharist was exposed) up for blessing. At that second, I felt as if someone was touching my tongue, and I started to praise God with the "gift of tongues." This is one of the first visible gift I got from Holy Spirit.

Suddenly I saw the heavens open with my eyes closed, and I saw a white dove coming down and touching me, and it turned into a ball of fire over me. I was completely immersed in it. This was one of the best heavenly experiences I ever had. Words could not express it, and I was shaking violently. Then I opened my eyes and everyone around was looking at me. I felt ashamed and tried to hold on to the chair in front of me. It was a steel chair, and it started to shake with me! This continued for a minute or two. When this stopped, I had no strength in me. I dropped to my knees and bowed down my head on floor and started to worship God. I enjoyed every moment of it.

After this experience, I felt like a feather floating in air, and there was a gushing of peace and joy in my heart. I knew then that Jesus has sealed me with his Holy Spirit, and I became a child of God.

Acts 2: 17, 18—"This is what I will do in the last days." God says, "I will pour out my spirit on everyone. Your sons and daughters will proclaim my message; your young men will see visions, and your old men will have dreams. Yes, even on my servants, both men and women, I will pour out my spirit in those days and they will proclaim my message."

CHAPTER 2

The Vision and the Wedding

When I started to walk with Jesus, I had many wonderful experiences. He started to teach me many things. Everyday, the Holy Spirit used to wake me up around 4:00 a.m. to pray. For the first time in my life, I started to wake up that early and pray. During this time, I would be filled with the Holy Spirit. When I started reading the Bible, the words came alive, and I spent hours in front of Bible studying and meditating. Best of all, the Holy Spirit helped me to understand everything.

As the days went by, I knew that God had enabled me to praise God in different tongues and also to sing in tongues. He opened my mind to discern what was right and what was wrong in God's sight—what was from God and what was from evil. Sometimes, I could even smell the presence of evil, and when I started to praise Jesus in tongues, the Evil Spirit would depart from me.

During these days, I understood that the Holy Spirit had poured out these gifts/charisms upon me from the retreat. They are the gift of vision, the gift of knowledge, the gift of understanding, the gift of healing, and the gift of prophesy.

There were visible signs of healings, like when my mom was sick and had a fever, I prayed to Jesus, and she was instantaneously healed. Another time, I prayed for my grandmother to be healed of her arm pain, and Jesus healed her. I felt as if I was in heaven to taste the heavenly gifts.

I used to visit a chapel near my workplace every day and spend time in front of Blessed Sacrament and pray. Then the Lord would come and talk to me from the Eucharist.

One day, while I was praying, a huge screen appeared in front of me. I was awestruck. On the screen, I saw many cities, then many mountains, forests, and deserts. Also, many nations appeared in front of me. I saw myself travelling through these cities, mountains, forests, and deserts on a horse. As I gazed at the screen, I was holding a sword in my hand and was riding the horse through many countries. Suddenly the screen disappeared. I was thrilled as well as confused at what I saw. While I was speculating what this meant, a woman came and stood in front of me. When I looked at her, I realized that was Mother Mary. I was breathless for a second. She was so beautiful and was wearing a long white dress and had a blue top over the shoulder and was holding a rosary. As I gazed at her in amazement, there were tears rolling down her cheeks. I became sad and asked her, "Mama, what happened."

She said, "Look at this."

When I looked towards her left, I saw the earth and saw millions of faces. They were all weeping and in pain. I saw the agony on their faces. Then I saw people with sicknesses and diseases. They were in wars and famines. People were crying for mercy and people were dying. When I saw this, tears started to roll out of my eyes. Mother Mary said, "I want you to pray the rosary for them."

I said, "Okay mother, I will do it." And she disappeared.

Suddenly I came to my senses. I couldn't believe what I had see and wanted to tell everyone that I seen Mother Mary. But then I thought *No one is going to believe me. Everybody is going to say I am crazy.* Seeing my changes, my friends had already started to make fun of me, and some of them had even left me. Everyone thought I was too religious. But that didn't stop me. I still loved my Lord and trusted him.

The following days, I was very confused about the vision. I thought I would ask the parish priest, who I knew personally. But he could not answer me. Then I decided to ask the director of a retreat center near my workplace about the vision. He couldn't help me either. I was very disturbed about the vision. So I asked the Lord to explain the meaning about the vision, but my request was in vain. I didn't know where to turn to, so I kept on asking the Lord—for days at first, which turned to weeks.

All of this started to take a toll on me. I thought I was going crazy. Jesus was not talking to me as he had before. He had not been with me for weeks. I started to get upset, feeling as if he was ignoring me or abandoning me. I asked the Lord, "Where are you, Lord? Why don't you talk to me? Are you mad at me"? I kept on asking these questions, but there was no answer from him.

A few months went by. Everything went back to the previous ways. I felt as if I was not getting anywhere with this so-called spiritual life. Slowly I started to lose interest in spiritual things. I thought God was upset with me. I couldn't pray as I used to be. I lost interest in the Word of God. I didn't want to pray the rosary. These days I didn't feel like getting up early in the morning to go for Mass. I couldn't understand what was going on. I didn't realize that this was a small test on my faith.

Even though I couldn't feel him, I still tried to pray and keep up with my spiritual activities. One of my main prayers was "Lord, give me the answer for the vision. Explain it to me, Lord. Either come directly and explain it, or send someone to me." I prayed this for weeks.

One day my parents called me and said, "Someone is here to meet with you, so please come home." I was at my work in another district. I asked them who he was. They said, "He was sent by Lord to see you and talk to you." I felt very strange but surprised.

After work I went home to meet this person, whom God "had sent." When I walked in, I saw a fragile figure with beard, smiling at me. He introduced himself. He said, "I was travelling on bus through this area, and the Lord told me to get down at the bus stop and led me to this house to meet you." I was amazed at what he said.

My mom was preparing dinner for us, so I invited him to have dinner. But he said, "First I have to pray with you, and only after that will I eat or drink anything." I agreed. When he started giving praise, the power of God filled our house, and God opened my spiritual eyes to see more visions. I started to speak these visions out, and he provided the explanations for everything. I knew then that he was a prophet and sent by God. I was so happy that God had sent someone to answer my prayers. He stayed with us for two days. As he was leaving, I said, "Maybe the Lord wants me to be a priest for his church. That is why he blessed me with so many spiritual gifts." He said he did not know that, but he told me to do a partial fasting and prayer for fourteen days, and following this period, the Lord would answer me directly. I agreed. After this, he left.

When I was leaving for my workplace, I said to my parents, "I may choose the priesthood, so please pray for me," and I reminded my mom not to bring any marriage proposals.

During this period of fasting, on the thirteenth day, my mom called me and said, "There is a girl you should meet—the daughter of one of your dad's friends. If you are interested, we will go and meet her."

I got mad at my mom and told her, "Mom! You know what I am planning in my life—to be a priest! So don't bother me with these distractions. And please don't ever call me with these marriage proposals, period!"

That night, while I was praying, the Lord came near me. I was so happy to see him again. He looked at me, smiling, and said, "Listen to your mom. Call her; go and meet that girl."

I was shocked to hear it. I said to the Lord, "Mom will say things like this, but you know that I want to serve you all the time and dedicate my entire life for you. I would rather be a priest."

Now Lord was not smiling. He looked at me firmly and said, "Obey me."

But I offered more excuses. "Lord, you know that I don't know this girl. Moreover, I don't have any money in my bank account, and I am in debt. So how will I have money for the wedding?" Then Jesus quoted the scripture from Matthew 6:25–33: "This is why I tell you: do not be worried about the food and drink you need in order to stay alive, or about clothes for your body. After all, isn't life worth more than food? And isn't the body worth more than clothes? Look at the birds: they do not plant seeds, gather a harvest and put it in barns; yet your father in heaven takes care of them! Aren't you worth much more than birds? Can any of you live a bit longer by worrying about it?

"And why worry about clothes? Look how the wild flowers grow: they do not work or make clothes for themselves. But I tell you that not even king Solomon with all his wealth had clothes as beautiful as one of these flowers. It is God who clothes the wild grass—grass that is here today and gone tomorrow, burned up in the oven. Won't he be all the sure to clothe you? What little faith you have!

"So do not start worrying: 'where will my food come from? Or my drink? Or my clothes?' Your father in heaven knows that you need all these things. Instead, be concerned about everything else with the kingdom of God and with what he requires of you, and he will provide you with all these other things."

But I was still stubborn and would not listen to the Lord, so he turned back and started walking away from me. Suddenly, I felt like something had been lifted away from me. I became like a dead man. I realized that the Holy Spirit had left me. For the first time, I realized how I would be without Holy Spirit—lifeless, hopeless, and abandoned. I fell to my knees and started crying and called on Jesus to come back. I promised I would listen to him and will do whatever he asked of me. I cried to the Lord, as David cried in Psalms, "Lord, do not take away the Holy Spirit from me, but restore unto me the joy of your salvation."

Immediately the power of God came on me once again. Then the Lord said in an audible voice, "I want obedience rather than sacrifice."

That night, after my prayers, I was lying on the bed. Suddenly I went into a trance. My spirit was lifted out of me. I started to travel upwards, and I reached a place. I knew I was in Heaven. I started floating over a transparent blue glassy sea. As I was moving forward, I saw a river flowing towards my left, and I saw a tree with lots of green branches. The farther along I floated, the more peace and joy I felt. Then I realized something: I could see everything; I could hear everything and feel everything. As I moved forward, at a distance, I saw a great throne. From that throne, a dazzling light came and lit up the entire place. I knew then that was God, and I was filled with awe. As I kept on gazing at the throne, I saw twenty-four elders clothed in white worshiping God. I was awestruck by the whole experience. The feeling was unimaginable. While I was gazing in amazement, Jesus came near me and said, "Come with me." I started to follow him. Suddenly I started to fall downwards towards darkness. I tried to hold on to something, but there was nothing to hold on to. It was pitch black all around. I felt as if I had landed on something. Then I started to cry and look for help. I felt that I was at the edge of a cliff, hanging on to it. When I looked down, I was consumed with horror. I saw huge tongues of fire rising up and heard people screaming. I could see their faces. They were in anguish. I looked around and cried, "Lord, where are you? Lord I can't take this. I am dying." As I was holding on to this cliff, I was sweating immensely and was shaking. Suddenly I felt a hand on me, lifting me back up. Immediately I was back in my room, where my body was, but I couldn't believe my self. I was looking at my body lying on the bed from the ceiling. I tried to reenter my body, but I couldn't. Then I pleaded to the Lord, "Lord, please let me back into my body, and I will live for you."

I jumped out of the bed and looked at my body. I was covered with sweat and shaking severely. I tried to believe it had all been a dream. But it was not, and I kept everything in my heart.

Next day morning, I called my mom and said, "I will come and see the girl who you spoke about."

My mom was surprised to hear that. She asked, "How come you changed your mind so fast!"

This happened on a Friday, and I made arrangements to go and meet her on Saturday.

Actually, I never believed in arranged marriages. I always thought that if I was going to get married, I always wanted to date a girl first. But here I was, going to see a girl whom I had never met or spoken with, to ask her to marry me, because the Lord said so!

I could not digest the idea of getting married at the age of twenty-four. But I was scared of all the things I had seen the night before, and I definitely didn't want to go to hell by disobeying the Lord.

So, on Saturday, I set out to see my future "wife to be," wearing the worst outfit—an old torn jeans and a T-shirt, without shaving or combing my hair and with a flip flow (chapel) on. My dad came with me. On the way I thought, "What if that girl has some problems? What if she doesn't look good? What if she is handicapped?" But then suddenly I said to myself, "No no, my Lord wouldn't do that to me. If he gives me anything, he gives the best." So I trusted the Lord to give me a beautiful and wise wife!

When I met with her, I thanked God for giving me the most beautiful woman I had ever met. After our introduction, I got straight to the point. "Today I came to see you because Jesus told me so, and he wanted me to marry you!"

I was expecting her to turn down the proposal. Instead, she said, "Last night, I had a dream. An angel came to me and said, "Today someone will come to you and will say these words, and he will be your husband."

I gasped when I heard her say this, and suddenly I had goose bumps all over. I started praising God for everything and said sorry to the Lord for not trusting him.

On my way back home, I was thinking, "Am I still dreaming. Is this from the Lord, or is it from the devil?" When I arrived home, to my surprise, I saw the same person who interpreted the visions for me. As I approached him, he started saying, "There is a wedding to take place at this house, and it will happen in the beginning of next year."

I asked him, "Are you also coming from her house? Did you talk to them?"

He replied "No!" Then he said, "The Lord told me to come back and say these things to you so that you may believe."

Then he started to describe the features of their house and what color of paint they used inside the house and the features of my "wife-to-be." At that moment, tears started to roll from my eyes, and I said, "Lord, take away my unbelief."

The next day, Sunday afternoon, I went back to my workplace. On Monday afternoon, I got a phone call from my parents. They said, "Son, this is not going to work out for you. We will look for another girl.

I was breathless for a second. When I regained my strength, I asked them, "What happened?" My parents didn't give me any satisfactory explanation; they tried to change the topic. I asked, "But you are friends, aren't you? Moreover it's the Lord who told me to marry her."

Then my parents said, "They don't want to give their daughter to you anymore. It's over."

When I heard this, I went to my room, fell to my knees, and started crying. Then the Lord said, "Be of good courage. Do not be afraid. I am with you. Fight like a brave soldier against the evil one, and I will be with you."

So I got up and drove the car to the "father-in-law to be." I walked into his house and asked for his daughter's hand. I told him it was the Lord's will and I didn't care about anything else. I said, "The Lord has given me strength to work, and I will take care of your daughter."

With this he was happy and said, "If I am giving my daughter to anyone in this world, it will be you!"

I thanked the Lord for giving me the courage and wisdom to do everything. But when I reached home, my parents and relatives were upset with me and said they would not get involved in this wedding if I was marrying this girl.

But the Lord was with me. The prophet, like the person who came to see me, convinced my parents that it was God's will and not to go against it. Then everyone came together, and I received their support, and the wedding bells rang!

Habakkuk 2:2–4—"The Lord gave me this answer: 'Write down clearly on tablets what I reveal to you, so that it can be read at a glance. Put it in writing, because it is not yet time for it to come true. But the time is coming quickly, and what I show you will come true. It may seem slow in coming, but wait for it; it will certainly take place and it will not be delayed. And this is the message: Those who are evil will not survive, but the righteous will live by faith.'"

CHAPTER 3

The Prodigal Catholic

After coming to Canada in 1999, I started to hear lot of teachings about Bible from Protestant pastors and evangelists. I was impressed by their teachings, the way they explained the "word of God," the way the churches function, etc.

I was still going to a Catholic church near my house. I started to compare different Christian denominations and also started to visit different denominational churches, and I felt that the Catholic Church was very weak spiritually and almost "dead." I thought other Protestant churches in the community were vibrant, active, and strong in the "word of God." I felt that I was in the wrong place by going to Catholic Church, and I had to make a decision.

During this time, I started to question every teaching of the Catholic Church. I questioned child Baptism, confessing to a priest, priesthood, and religious nuns. I also had doubts about the teachings on Mother Mary, the rosary, purgatory, and on and on …

I found fault in everything the Catholic Church did.

In the year 2000, I left the Catholic Church and started going to a Pentecostal church. I wanted to get closer to God and know more about my Lord Jesus and worship him openly and freely. So I thought the Pentecostal Church would be better than Catholic Church. I thought as well, "They are so lively."

The Pentecostal Church welcomed me warmly. I met the pastor and met with lots of people. Everyone seemed to be enjoying every moment at this particular church. They were hugging, laughing, and praising the Lord. Everyone prayed in tongues! Everyone worshiped God. I thought this was the perfect place for me, and I thanked God. I completely stopped praying the rosary. I thought the Bible was enough. In my ignorance, I didn't realize the rosary was the Word of God. I put away all the Catholic literatures and the rosary. I even I took the rosary out of my car! And hid everything so that I should not see it. I said to myself, "Maybe I am getting little closer to God and know Jesus better now. I stopped using the Catholic Bible and started using other Bibles.

A few months went by. I started to feel that it was not the same as I had thought. I felt as if people were putting on a different face at church and outside. They were more fake than real. I heard pastors and preachers teaching more about financial blessings and tithing. They taught more on prosperity and blessings and very little about the cross and sufferings. It seemed as if people were trying to run away from reality. I thought this church wasn't living up to the Lord 100 percent, as they claim. There was something missing in this church. Above all, they were making fun of the Catholic Church and Mother Mary. That hurt me. I felt like they were mocking my mother. I tried to explain to them, "At least give the respect you give to your own mother." But it was in vain!

Slowly I started to withdraw from that church. For some time I didn't go to any church. I felt guilty and didn't go back to the Catholic Church. I started to pray to God and asked him to lead me to the right church, one that followed Jesus' footsteps and that followed the Bible 100 percent. I prayed earnestly for weeks, but God didn't give me an answer right away.

One day, while I was praying, a couple came to the house and said they were Witnesses of God. I welcomed them home. They started to come to my house more often and started to teach my wife and me about their church. They told me that they were the true followers of the Living God and followed Jesus Christ 100 percent. This couple gave us a bible and booklets to read. Their bible was different from other bibles. The verses were different. Also the interpretations differed. This made me more confused. I thought all the Bibles were same and contained the same meaning.

I started asking the couple questions about the Holy Spirit and the work of the Holy Spirit in salvation and healings (as I had been healed before).

They said the Holy Spirit was not a person in the Trinity, but it was the power of God. and the Holy Spirit didn't function now! They said, "The power of Holy Spirit was there when the Apostles were alive, and after their death, that power ended." Another thing they said was there was no Trinity. According to their teaching, "There is one and only God the father, and Jesus Christ was his only son," but he didn't share the same equality and same glory of God the Father. Jesus was like a smaller god, a second in command. But they believed in salvation. I could not understand everything they said. During this time, I took all my rosary, pictures of Jesus and Mary, and crucifix and threw them in garbage because, according to their teachings, they were all statues and hindrances against the direct relationship with the Father God.

As I studied their teachings and read through their Bible, I discovered many contradictions with other churches, especially the Catholic Church. After a few months, I had second thoughts about following them, and deep down I wanted to come back to the Catholic Church. By then I thought it would be too hard for me to come back, and I felt unworthy. For the first time, I wanted to go and cry at the altar of the Lord. I said, "I want to make a good confession. I will ask the priest whether I can come back to the Church and receive Communion."

One night, as I was thinking about these things in the living room, I heard a scream from the bedroom. My wife and my son were sleeping in the room at the time. I tried to wake my wife up, but she was in deep sleep. I felt there was someone in the room. I sensed the presence of evil in the room. Again, my wife started to grumble and started swearing and grinding her teeth. I knew that the Evil Spirit was attacking my wife. I started to call on the attributes of God, but nothing happened. I started to rebuke the Evil Spirit in the name of Jesus, but it was still attacking my wife. By now I started to sweat and wanted to cry. There was no one to help me. My wife was still in deep sleep. Suddenly I remembered Mother Mary, and slowly I said, "Hail Mary, full of grace, the Lord is with you. Blessed are you among women, and blessed is the fruit of your womb, Jesus." Immediately, to my utter amazement the Evil Spirit left my wife and went away. I started to weep. Then I knelt beside the bed and prayed the entire rosary. I asked pardon and forgiveness from the Lord and Mother Mary, and I promised that I would go back to Catholic Church and never leave the Church again.

At that moment, my wife woke up and asked me what happened. I said, "Everything is fine, dear."

She said, "Everything will be all right" and went back to sleep!

The next day was a Sunday. After two years, for the first time, I decided to go for a Holy Mass at a nearby Catholic Church. I didn't know it was the feast of "the body and blood of Christ," in other words, "Corpus Christi." During the Holy Mass, when the priest lifted up the Blessed Host and said, "This is the lamb of God who takes away the sin of the world," suddenly a bright light, like fire, came from the Blessed Host and hit me. I felt the mighty presence of God, and I knelt down and started to worship the Lord. From that day on, I never turned back from my Catholic Church, and I professed my faith, saying:

"I believe if God, the Father almighty, creator of heaven and earth. I believe in Jesus Christ, his only son, our Lord. He was conceived by the power of the Holy Spirit and born of the Virgin Mary. He suffered under Pontius Pilate, was crucified, died, and was buried. He descended into hell. On the third day he rose again. He ascended into heaven and is seated at the right hand of God the Father. He will come again to judge the living and the dead. I believe in the Holy Spirit, the holy Catholic Church, the communion of saints, the forgiveness of sins, the resurrection of the body, and life everlasting. Amen."

CHAPTER 4

The Tithe

We moved into our condominium in 2003, after the birth of our older daughter. Within few months of residing there, we ran into great financial struggles. At the time, I was the sole bread earner, because my wife stayed home, taking care of two children. I had a hard time in paying the mortgage, car loan, and other bills. Tension started to rise in our family. We were struggling to keep up with our livelihood.

During this time I started to pray earnestly to the Lord for a breakthrough in our finances and for abundant blessing. When I prayed, I claimed the promises in the Bible and remembered the past blessings He had showered on me. About this time, I used to listen to Christian TV channels and radio programs. In these programs, the preachers and pastors keep repeating about the financial blessings happening through their churches, and they taught mostly about tithing from the Bible, from the book of Malachi. When I listened to these sermons, as a Catholic, I thought, What does Catholic Church teach about this matter of tithing? I had never heard about any Catholic priests preaching about financial blessings and prosperity. I had heard many times about physical healings, inner healings, healing in relationships, and so on. For example, I myself was physically healed at the retreat center. I had also heard about giving time to the Lord, but not much about tithing. Then I thought, should we Catholics give our tithes to these other churches to be blessed?

I said to myself, "What happens to all those Catholics who go through financial struggles? Is it God's will for us to struggle like this, or is there a way out? Doesn't God want us Catholics to be blessed? Does he want us to live in poverty?" But when I read the Bible, contrary to my thoughts, I saw God's blessing throughout the Bible—God blessing Abraham, Isaac, and Jacob. God blessing Job and restoring everything he had lost, back seven fold. God blessing David and Solomon and the people of Israel. Then I started asking the Lord, "What is your will for me and all the Catholics who are struggling in the area of the finances?"

One day, as I was meditating on the word of God, I was going through the book of Hebrews, reading verses 7:1–2—"This Melchizedek was king of Salem and a priest of the Most High God. As Abraham was coming back from the battle in which he defeated the four kings, Melchizedek met him and blessed him and Abraham gave him one tenth of all he had taken." Suddenly the Holy Spirit led me to the book of Genesis, chapter 14:17–20—"When Abram came back from his victory over Chedorlaomer and other kings, the king of Sodom went out to meet him in Shaveh Valley. And Melchizedek, who was king of Salem and also a priest of the Most High God, brought bread and wine to Abram, blessed him and said, 'May the Most High God, who made heaven and earth, bless Abram! May the Most High God, who gave you victory over your enemies, be praised!' and Abram gave Melchizedek a tenth of all the loot he had recovered."

Suddenly the words "bread and wine" stuck in my mind. This sounded like the bread and wine in the Holy Mass. Then the Holy Spirit took me back to the book of Hebrews 5:6—"You will be a priest forever, in the priestly order of Melchizedek," and verse 7:3, where it says, "He is like the Son of God, he remains a priest forever." Also, I remembered this part being said in the Holy Mass.

Then it again says in the book of Hebrew 7:6 that Melchizedek was not descended from Levi, but he collected one tenth from Abraham and blessed him, the man who received God's promises. "There is no doubt that the one who blesses is greater than the one who is blessed."

When I read these verses, I started praising God for opening my mind and hearing my cry. As St. Ambrose said, "The bread and wine is transformed to the body and blood of Christ Jesus."

The priest who offered this bread and wine at the altar is transformed himself to the great high priest Jesus Christ, through the power of the Holy Spirit, and the bread and wine is transformed to Jesus's body and blood. I thought that the words in the book of Genesis foreshadowed the present-day Church (the descendent of Abraham by faith), and I recalled priests who offered the sacrifices at the altar through the priestly order of Melchizedek, and not through the Levitical priesthood. Now I remembered that we come before the altar to give ourselves and what we have, and the priest takes that and gives us the bread and wine, which is the body and blood of our Lord Jesus and blesses us as Melchizedek blessed Abraham.

Then the Holy Spirit led me to Malachi 3:6–12:

> I am the Lord, and I do not change. And so you, the descendants of Jacob, are not yet completely lost. You, like your ancestors before you, have turned away from my laws and have not kept them. Turn back to me, and I will turn to you. But you ask, "What must we do to turn back to you?" I ask you, "Is it right for a person to cheat God?" Of course not, yet you are cheating me. How? You ask. In the matter of tithes and offerings. A curse is on all of you because the whole nation is cheating me. Bring the full amount of your tithes to the temple, so that there will be plenty of food there. Put me to the test and you will see that I will open the windows of heaven and pour out on you in abundance all kinds of good things. I will not let insects destroy your crops and your grape vines will be loaded with grapes. Then the people of all nations will call you happy, because your land will be a good place to live.

I thanked the Lord for the word he gave me. As days went by, I started to think, how will I give my tenth to the Lord right now, as it is too hard for us to make ends meet? One day, while I was driving to work, the Lord spoke to me. "Sell the condominium, and I will give you a house."

I said, "Lord, you are kidding. I can't afford to pay for my condominium. How will I be able to pay for my house?" He said to trust him and have faith in him. Then I remembered how he walked me through the time of my wedding, and I believed in him. As it says in the book of James, "Faith without action is dead."

So I decided to act in faith and sold my condominium and put in an offer for a house. But this house was not in the will of God. Just one week before moving into this house, the sellers breached the contract and said they were not selling it anymore. By this time, we had sold our condominium, and we had to move. We moved into a rented house, and I paid off all my credit card bills.

Our mortgage was still on hold, as it was pre-approved from the previous house purchase. We started to look for another house to fit our budget and to be in line with the mortgage amount that had been pre-approved.

During this time, I got into a car accident, and whatever money I had left, I had to use to pay off the accident. I thought, *Maybe this is not the right time to buy a house. I will wait.* But the Lord said again to trust him and he would provide us with a house! I believed in the Lord and started to look for a house. I found the right house, which the Lord wanted me to have. I came to know that the family who wanted to sell the house had to sell it quick and also that my mortgage offer was expiring within a week.

But now a problem remained. I had to find the money for the down payment, which was $12,000 CAD, in addition to other expenses. I didn't have a penny in my bank account!

I cried to the Lord, "Lord, where am I going to get that much money?"

The money that I was supposed to get from back from India was stuck for some unknown reason.

Then the Holy Spirit reminded me what he had taught me from the book of Hebrews and about tithing. Also, it says in the book of Malachi "to test the Lord in this matter." So I decided to act in faith.

There was a Catholic Church nearby where we rented. It was a Monday, and my closing for the new house was on Friday of that same week. I decided to go for the evening Mass and to offer a check for CAD $120 to the priest and ask for his blessing. This was 10 percent of my gross pay for two weeks of work. During the Holy Mass, when the priest lifted up the host and wine towards heaven, I offered my intention with it. After the Mass, we went over to the priest and gave him this check and requested him to pray for us that the Lord might give us enough money to buy the house. He looked at me in surprise, but he agreed.

We started packing everything and got ready to move to our new house! On the same week Thursday, I got a phone call from back home saying that the money being held from a land transaction had been released and they were sending it over to us here in Canada. And it was exactly $12,000 CAD. I cried, jumping up saying, "Praise the Lord."

I suddenly remembered the promise of God in Malachi 3:10: "Bring the full amount of your tithes to the temple so that there will be plenty of food there. Put me to the test and you will see that I will open the windows of heaven and pour out on you in abundance all kinds of good things." Amen.

CHAPTER 5

The Lord's Coming

In the year 2005, as I was going through the book of Daniel and Revelation, it came to my mind, *Am I ready to receive Lord Jesus if he comes right now? Is my family ready to receive him? Is my church ready? How much knowledge do we have about his second coming?* Then I realized that our church didn't talk much about Lord's return. The only time I heard about it was during the yearly advent season, when we went through the book of Revelation quickly, without much explanation. It is also in the Apostle's Creed, where it says, "He will come again to judge the living and the dead." But I never really noticed this part or cared about it until one day, during the month of September, when I was at home. I was sick and didn't go to work that day. I was lying on the couch in our family room and was thinking and praying about his coming. It was around 3pm in the afternoon, and I started slowly singing the Divine Mercy Chaplet. During the Chaplet, I asked the Lord, "Lord, how deep was your pain at Calvary, and how much agony did you go through on the cross?"

As I was thinking about this, I was singing the Chaplet with my eyes closed. Suddenly, I saw St. Faustina sitting next to me and singing the Chaplet with me. I jumped off the couch, terrified, seeing her. When I regained my breath, I asked her in amazement, "How did you know the pain of Lord Jesus so intensely and know about his mercy?"

She told me, "Come with me to Calvary, and we will do the Chaplet there."

She took me in the spirit to Calvary, and we started to sing the divine mercy. Suddenly, I saw the Lord Jesus carrying the cross. I saw the soldiers, whipping and beating Jesus. I saw women crying. I saw people screaming. I saw horses neighing. I couldn't bear the pain. I fell on the floor, wailing. I said to St. Faustina, "Let's go back. I can't take this. I can't see my Lord being whipped and beaten. I will die in grief if I am here."

But she said, "I want you to know how much he loved you, how much he gave for the Church so that everyone may know about his love and mercy."

I couldn't sing the Chaplet more. I was just weeping. But St. Faustina started singing the Divine Mercy Chaplet. She took hold of me, and we started to walk with Jesus through the streets and towards Calvary. It was extremely painful and agonizing. I came to know how much Jesus loved me, shedding his blood and life to save me. His mercy was like a sea.

This went on for two hours, and once the Chaplet was over, St. Faustina left me. I was still lying on the floor weeping. Suddenly I saw a huge serpent crawling towards me. I knew it was Satan. I got very angry at Satan. I shouted at him, "How could you keep us away from the love of the Lord?" I got hold of his neck and said, "I rebuke you, Satan, in the precious name of the Lord Jesus." And threw him away from me. Then Satan left me.

Suddenly, I saw mother Mary. She touched me and lifted me up to my knees. My sickness left me, and I regained some strength! As I was kneeling, she told me to pray the rosary for the whole world. When I started to pray the rosary, the Lord took me again in the spirit around the world. I started to pray for each continent. I saw the ailing Africa, with famine all around, with diseases and wars and pestilences. I saw the Asia, with ignorance about the Lord and worshipping other gods. I saw the wars in the Middle East. I saw a godless world, people being too materialistic—Europe, North America, and Australia, not allowing the Lord to change them.

As I was watched all these people in darkness, I was back in my room and started to intercede for them in rosary. This went on for more than an hour. Towards the end of the rosary, again the Lord took me in the spirit to the end times. The Lord said, "This is what's going to happen just before my return." I couldn't believe what I saw. I saw terrible earthquakes. I saw chaos in every city in the world, and I saw huge buildings crumbling down. I saw huge traffic jams everywhere. People trying to get out of cities, people running around screaming. I saw people falling from huge buildings. I saw seas coming up, roaring towards land. I saw roads and bridges cracking and falling down.

At that very moment, I saw the sky open and huge locusts, as big as a horse, coming down and attacking human beings and animals. They had sharp teeth and large claws, and they were eating the flesh of human beings and animals. Then I remembered, these were not like the locusts I had read about in the book of Exodus. These were huge and eating men. I was struck with horror. I saw total darkness covering the earth during midday and the moon turning red at night. Suddenly I remembered what it says in the book of Joel 2:30–32—"I will give warnings of that day in the sky and on the earth; there will be bloodshed, fire and clouds of smoke. The sun will be darkened, and the moon will turn red as blood, before the great and terrible day of the Lord comes. But all who ask the Lord for help will be saved. As the Lord has said, 'Some in Jerusalem will escape. Those whom I choose will survive.'"

This happened when I was alone at home, and it went on for another two hours. I was very disturbed and kept everything in my heart. I was thinking, "Who can escape the wrath of God?" This made me very upset.

The next day again, as I was thinking about the incidents that happened the previous day, the Lord told me to take the Bible, and he led me to 1 Thessalonica 5:1–11.

There is no need to write you, friends, about the times and occasions when these things will happen. For you yourselves know very well that the Day of the Lord will come as a thief comes at night. When people say, "Everything is quiet and safe," then suddenly destruction will hit them! It will come as suddenly as the pain that come upon a woman in labor, and people will not escape. But you, friends, are not in the darkness, and the Day should not take you by surprise, like a thief. All of you are people who belong to the light, who belong to the day. We do not belong to the night or to the darkness. So then, we should not be sleeping like the others; we should be awake and sober. It is at night when people sleep; it is at night when they get drunk. But we belong to the day, and we should be sober. We must wear faith and love as breastplate, and our hope of salvation as a helmet. "God did not choose us to suffer his anger, but to possess salvation through our Lord Jesus Christ, who died for us in order that we might live together with him, whether we are alive or dead when he comes." And so encourage one another and help one another, just as you are now doing.

And I said, "Maranatha, come, Lord Jesus."

CHAPTER 6

Abba Father

God so loved the world that he gave his only begotten son, so that who shall ever believes in him will not perish but have everlasting life.

—John 3:16

I always wanted to know the depths of God's love, as it says in the Bible. It is as a father's love for his children, or more than that. Throughout the Bible, God mentions his love through different examples and parables. If we read the Bible from Genesis to Revelation, we will see his love mentioned many times, from the beginning of creation, from our first parents, Adam and Eve, how God wants to pour his love on them and associate with them. Then, after that, we see how he loved Abel, Enoch, Noah, Abraham, Isaac, Jacob, Joseph, Moses, and the children of Israel. Then we see that love again through King David and Solomon, through the Psalms and the Song of Songs or the Song of Solomon, how God's love is revealed to us as a lover who wants to pour out his love to his beloved. Also through the prophets, how we see God loves us and wants to carry us in his arms. It is the same way a chicken carries her young ones, how a shepherd carries a wounded sheep.

At the end, he revealed his love for us through the Gospels, Epistles, and Revelation, by sending his only son, Jesus Christ, to show a father's love for us through his teachings and his ministry. At the end, he died on a cross for us to show his *agape* love, the ultimate sacrifice on the cross, by shedding his precious blood, to redeem us and bring back to himself. And finally, in the Revelation, the Lord will come back as a bridegroom to bring back his bride, the Church, to himself, for where he is we shall be too with him, for eternity.

For me, I always wanted to know the depths of the love of God, as Jesus says in the Gospels. Even after coming to know Jesus more personally, through the retreat, and having the outpouring of Holy Spirit in my life, with signs and wonders, I was still lacking the depth and knowledge of Father's love for me.

John 3:16 became one of my favorite verses in the bible. I tried to meditate on this verse every day through the year 2005. I used to listen to the teachings and sermons on this verse. Even though I tried to understand the depth of this verse, I couldn't fully grasp the meaning of it. I keep asking God, "Please take me to the depth of this Bible passage, John 3:16."

One of the toughest periods of my life was when my wife was pregnant and carrying our twin babies. During their fifth month, her water broke and with complications she was admitted to hospital. The doctors said she would deliver the babies any minute. They prepared us to be ready if the babies didn't live. I couldn't do anything but cry to the Lord for help. My wife was crying, and when I saw her tears, I couldn't bear it. At that moment, I felt that I couldn't even pray, and my faith was shattered. I just started to say, *Jesus, Jesus, Jesus …*

When she was taken to the operation theatre, I could not hold on to myself. I called a few of my friends and asked for prayer. I felt that I was walking on burning coals.

A few hours went by, and the doctors came back and said, "She is not delivering babies now. Her birth pain is gone. We will see what will happen in next day or two." She was moved to a semi-private room. I thanked the Lord, saying, "At least the babies are okay now!"

It was a time of great test for us. We could expect anything any minute. We didn't know what to do but kept praying for the babies and mom. Doctors and nurses came and said, "There is not much hope. It is better to abort them. It will be safer for mother." We got pressure from every side, even from our families. But we didn't want to abort the babies. I told the doctors and nurses that as Catholics we would not abort the babies but wait until their natural death.

It was a tough choice. We were preparing ourselves for anything, either death or life of our babies. Every day after work, I visited my wife at the hospital. When I got back home, I wouldn't get sleep, and I knelt beside my bed and cried to the Lord to save the life of the babies. I used to pray the psalms, and they comforted me and strengthened me.

Almost every day, the hospital staff took ultrasounds of the babies, and we were amazed to see them alive and well in the womb. That gave us confidence. My wife did her best to keep the pregnancy until full term. I thought, as Psalms 23 says, we were literally walking through the valley of the shadow of death. This continued for almost a month.

When the doctors found out that my wife had entered her sixth month of pregnancy, they thought they could save the lives of babies. They send her to the specialist hospital in downtown Toronto. This hospital handled babies born prematurely and with complications, and our hope also increased by seeing the faith of doctors in saving the lives of the babies. Without any warning, my wife went into labor and delivered the babies within a few days of reaching the hospital.

When she was in labor, I was at work. The nurse called me at work and said, "Your wife delivered the babies, and they are fine." I couldn't believe that. I was thrilled to hear the babies were alive and well, but when I reached hospital, the situation was different. The first baby she delivered (we named him Samuel) had problems breathing. Even in ventilator he couldn't breathe, because his lungs hadn't fully developed. He died after five hours of his birth, around 5:00 p.m. Even though we were prepared for anything, we still didn't want this to happen. We wept as he left us. When I took him in my arms, I couldn't believe myself. He was fully grown, with long hands and legs with lots of hair on his head!

We came back to the hospital room and had our supper around 10:00 p.m. We were still thankful that God spared Nathaniel, and he was doing well. All the doctors and nurses assured that he would be fine, even though he was in the NICU. All the staff at the hospital were happy for us that at least one baby was alive. After a few hours, the doctor came to our room. When I looked at him, he was shaking and his words were trembling. He said that Nathaniel's health was deteriorating. A chill went up my spine.

When I looked at my wife's face, she looked frozen; there were no tears left to cry. I started to cry in my heart. I said, "No, Lord, you can't take him. Won't you at least spare him? We can't handle him being taken away. Please, Lord, you can't do this. Don't you see my heart? Don't you see a dad's pain!"

Against all odds, God did what seemed right in his eyes. After eleven hours of struggle, God took him.

So, on December 21, 2005, we lost our twin children, Samuel and Nathaniel. My wife and I went through grieving during this period. When I was in deep pain, I asked these questions to God. "God, why did it happen to us? What did we do to get this?" I couldn't imagine that we had to go through something like this in our lifetime. I couldn't bear the pain.

The funeral for the babies was on December 26, 2005. As it was the Christmas season, during those days when I went to church, it was hard to keep the emotions in check. Everywhere there were songs about baby Jesus, and everyone was enjoying their holidays. One day, while I was at Holy Mass, I was wondering whether our parents could be here to help us and be with us. I suddenly felt there were no family or relatives here to help us and support us other than our friends, and I couldn't bear the pain anymore. Suddenly I saw mother Mary and Jesus coming down from the altar. Mother Mary hugged me and started to cry with me, and Jesus also embraced me. I wouldn't ever forget this experience. I poured out my grief upon them. It was as if heavenly family members were consoling me. While I was at church, my wife took rest at home. She needed to be healed of her body.

It became a big scar in my heart. I was upset and angry with God. I started questioning God, "Aren't you a loving father? Aren't you a God who heals us? Aren't you our provider? Then why did you take away our children from us? Why did you give them to us in the first place just to take them away?"

Over the next few months, I started to hear a voice say, "God doesn't love you enough? Otherwise, he would have spared your children, and you wouldn't have gone through such pain. See, he doesn't care for you. He took everything from you." I slowly started to hate myself and started to hate God too, since I thought he didn't love me anymore.

One day, as I was reading John 3:16, I felt like those verses suddenly started to come alive. I started to weep vigorously. When I read again, I interpreted the verses as, "For God so loved 'me' that he gave his only begotten son for 'me,' and if I believe in him I will not perish but have eternal life.

Suddenly I felt the presence of the Lord. He came near me and hugged me. I started to weep even louder. During this time, I was alone in the house. My wife was at work. At that moment, I asked Jesus a question. "Do you know the pain of a father!" Jesus looked at me and said, "Listen to my father."

Then I heard an audible voice saying to me, "My son, do you know how much I love you? It's there in your favorite verse. Don't you see my love poured out for you and for all humanity in these words? Do you know how much pain I went through when they nailed my son to the cross? I was in tears looking at my child. That was for you, my son."

Then I wept and called out to God the Father, "Pappa, my Pappa." That is how I call my dad. Then he said, "The babies are safe with me. Everyone belongs to me. I am the father to all my children."

I asked my heavenly father by making a request, "Pappa, will you show me the babies whenever I want to see them in spirit?" He agreed. Now I see them and feel them as little angels when I long to see them—with my spiritual eyes and also in the blessed adoration and prayer for the dead.

From that time onward, I had the father's presence and love for me. Now that John 3:16 came alive in me, whenever I fell (sin), I felt so unworthy for the Father's love.

But the Holy Spirit led me to the parable of the prodigal son, Luke 15:11–32. It is one of the greatest love stories ever told, a story filled with mercy and grace. It is a parable of how God views us and how we can choose to repent and turn to God or reject him.

At times I consider myself as the younger son, who ran away with his inheritance and spend it on foolish things, finding myself in the pig hole and coming to my senses at the age of twenty-three. I returned home, saying to my heavenly father that I was not worthy of his love and not able to call myself his son. But he doesn't listen to me. He tells his servants, his angels, to bring the robe of righteousness and wear me. He removes the ring from his finger and puts that on my finger as the mark of son-ship and gives me the sandals to wear as a mark of kingship.

Where did that righteousness come from? Where did that son-ship come from? Where did that kingship come from? From Calvary, from the cross. By shedding his son's precious blood. It says in Isaiah 64:6, "What are we? Nothing. What is our righteousness? They are like dirty rags. So where did that righteousness come from. It is from the precious blood of our Lord Jesus. As it says in the scripture (Romans 5:8), "While we were yet sinners he died for us."

The image that comes to my mind is that of the prodigal son. The father comes out every day looking for the son, to see whether he is coming home, to take him back, to show his love and mercy. In the same way, our heavenly Father waits for each of us sinners, to love us unconditionally and even before we could open our mouth and say sorry to him in the confessional, he will pour out his love over us and be proud of us as his children and co-brothers and co-sisters of his son Jesus. The heavens rejoice when a sinner comes back home to his or her heavenly daddy, to be in constant communion with the Father, to know the will of the Father for us in this life, to know the purpose of our life on this earth.

As always, Jesus, as our perfect example, is constantly seeking the will of the Father. He is in constant fellowship and communion with the Father. So, brothers and sisters, let us follow Jesus Christ, the perfect example, as our Lord, brother, and friend, to know our heavenly father, to grow in his love and to work towards his kingdom.

My saving power will rise on you like the sun.

—Malachi 4:2

CHAPTER 7

Anointing in Dubai

In March 2008, I lost my job. This was the first time in Canada I didn't have a job. My family was back home at the time. My wife was going to university there, and she was studying for bachelor in education.

I was very upset about the loss of my job, but I started looking for other jobs. It was very hard to find a job I wanted with the same salary and position I held before. This was the recession in North America. Everywhere companies were cutting down on staff, and people were being laid off. I had to prepare mentally myself for this new situation and my all-around negativity. I started to pray to the Lord and go to Holy Mass every day. God gave me strength through prayers. During those days, when I felt discouraged, I remembered the promises of God and proclaimed the scriptures in Bible when I went for a walk or drive. A few of my favorite verses were as follows:

- Psalms 23:1—"The Lord is my shepherd; I shall not want."
- Jeremiah 29:11—"I alone know the plans I have for you, plans to bring you prosperity and not disaster, plans to bring about the future you hope for."
- Luke 1:37—"For there is nothing that God cannot do."

These promises gave me courage and strength. I also liked to pray the rosary every day. One day, as I was praying my rosary, Mother Mary started to talk to me in an audible voice. I was thrilled to hear her voice.

She said, "Lord has kept a blessing for you in Dubai. He is going to pour his spirit upon you once again." Then I saw a vision of Dubai. I saw I was reaching Dubai, but to my surprise, I was going on a ship, and I was standing on the deck. When the ship was reaching closer to the Dubai port, I saw all the tall buildings were bowing down to me.

I was amazed at the sight, and I was also thrilled. I thought, "God is going to give me a beautiful job there, and also he is going to fill me with his Holy Spirit. Hallelujah"!

Then I started to search for jobs in Dubai on internet. As my profession was hotel management, I started to look for employment in the top five-star hotels. One of the hotel groups was Juma. I sent my resumes over there and talked to human resources at few hotels under the Juma Group. The HR manager at Palm Juma gave me positive feedback and said if I am coming to Dubai, he would definitely like to meet with me for an interview. When I heard this, I was happy, and I thought everything was working according to my plan. I was planning to go back home to meet my family, so I thought I would stay in Dubai for a week and get the job and head home and when I returned to Canada I would pack up my stuff and head back to Dubai. I said, "Praise the Lord."

I got the ticket for India via Dubai and boarded the flight with lots of dreams. I landed in Dubai and stayed with my friend. This was the second time I had been in an Arab country. My first visit was when I was in grade eight, when my dad was working there. When I reached Dubai, the first thing I did was call this HR manager I had talked to, over the phone from Canada. After first few words, he said, "I am sorry, you are not a suitable candidate for this position because most of your experience is in restaurant chains and we need a candidate who has five-star hotel experience."

When I heard this, I was very upset. I said to the Lord, "Lord, I thought you brought me here to give me a good job at one of the five-star hotels here and have a beautiful life. Why did this happen to me?" I was so sure I would get this job at Palm Juma, and my eyes were wet. But the Lord didn't answer me. I started to look for other jobs, but nothing came through right away. I was very upset with the Lord. I thought, "I came here as per God's guidance to get a job, and now I am in limbo."

I thought, anyway, here I am. I will go and meet some of the Charismatic leaders at the Catholic Church in Dubai. When I reached there, I couldn't meet anyone, so I left a message with a priest at the church, requesting to meet a particular person at the Charismatic movement. I was upset about the whole trip to Dubai. I thought, *It's already been five days in Dubai, and I haven't achieved anything here, neither any jobs nor any blessing from Lord.*

Then I thought, *Did Mother Mary really speak to me, or was it someone else?* I kept everything in my heart and didn't say anything to anyone.

I called my aunt in Dubai. I met her there on the fifth day. After our initial conversation, she said she was into the Charismatic movement. I was surprised to hear that. I asked her, "So, are you going to this Charismatic prayer group at the Catholic Church in Dubai?"

She said, "No, I am going to a movement called SRM, and it's in Sharjah."

I was surprised to hear about this new movement. She invited me to this group, which gathered every Thursdays at this church in Sharjah, UAE.

At first I was skeptical about this group. I thought, "A different group from the Charismatic group in the Catholic Church!" I was surprised. I didn't want to say no to my aunt, who had enthusiastically invited me to their group, so I agreed to visit there on Thursday. It was my sixth day in Dubai.

I thought, "I have one more day left here in Dubai. What a waste of time here!" But I tried to encourage myself, "Anyway, I got to see Dubai, meet many people, see the country, travel through the streets, ride in cabs, walk through the dusty roads, and meet some Arabs!" I had never seen traffic anywhere like this. On the highway, some Arabs stopped their cars in the middle of the road just to get out of the car and go do something else, causing huge traffic jams!

So, on Thursday, I went to this church in Sharjah, to this so-called group SRM. When I arrived there, their prayer had already started, and to my surprise, I saw three interconnecting rooms filled with people. There were roughly 150 people crammed into those three rooms. I went into the second room. There were mini TVs in each room, showing the live praise and worship. Soon the hallway started to fill. I thought "Wow, there should be something amazing here. So many people fill this place! There should be a real presence of the Lord here."

During the service, I saw a lady leading the praise and worship session.

I had never seen anyone praising God with this power. When she praised God, there was a mighty anointment filling the place. After the service, my aunt took me to meet this lady and another gentleman who preached the "Word of God." For some reason, I was reluctant to meet with them, so I went downstairs to have a cup of tea. My aunt came down to me and compelled me to meet with them. When I came upstairs, where the meeting was held, the gentleman who preached the Word of God was on his way out. My aunt introduced me to him at the doorway. He was in a hurry so he left. I came inside the hall with my aunt, and she introduced me to this lady. She looked at me and held my hand tight.

"You need to leave your prejudice," she said, "and sometimes you have to go after the anointed people to get their anointing. It should be like Elisha following Elijah for the anointing."

I looked at her and I thought that she knew what had happened here: I didn't want to meet up with them. In my mind, I still thought I had to meet up with someone in the Charismatic group to get the anointing of the Holy Spirit, as said by Mother Mary.

The lady was still holding my hand and looked at me. "This evening, we will meet at your aunt's place and pray." I agreed and I left.

Later in the afternoon, this lady and my aunt came to pick me up from my friend's house. We came to my aunt's house. I knew something mighty was going to happen. When we started to praise, a mighty presence of God filled the room. Suddenly, the power of the Holy Spirit came upon me. I was shaking violently! Now I was not embarrassed. I enjoyed every moment of it. My spiritual eyes were opened, and I saw all the visions I saw when I prayed with this particular gentleman ten years, back in 1998, when he came to meet me for the first time. My heart was filled with joy. I started to laugh and cry in the spirit. I was in a state of drunkenness in the spirit.

Then the Lord enabled me to prophesy over the nations. The Lord said, "He will touch the hearts of people in this land. There will be mighty conversations and he will be using us and the SRM group as his instruments in converting these nations. There will be a mighty protection and intercession from Mother Mary."

Thus, I left Dubai with a double portion of anointing.

Luke 1—"You are the most blessed of all women, and blessed is the child you will bear!"

Luke 45—"How happy you are to believe that the Lords message to you will come true!"

Mary's song of Praise

Luke 1:46–55

Mary said,

"My heart praises the Lord;
My soul is glad because of
God my Savior,
For he has remembered me,
His lowly servant!
From now on all people will call
Me happy,
Because of the great things
The Mighty God has
Done for me.
His name is holy;
From one generation to another
He shows mercy to those who
Honor him.
He has stretched out his
Mighty arm
And scattered the proud with
All their plans.
He has brought down mighty
Kings from their thrones,
And lifted up the lowly.
He has filled the hungry with
Good things,
And sent, the rich away with
Empty hands

He has kept the promise he
Made to our ancestors
And has come to the help of
His servant Israel.
He has remembered to show
mercy to Abraham
and to all his descendants
forever!"

And I said, "Amen."

CHAPTER 8

The Living Faith

If your faith is not enduring, you will not endure.

—Isiah 7:9

After the encounter with the Lord, in September 1998, I was very active in many ministries, especially in the youth ministry. Near my workplace, there was a retreat center where I used to give talks and share my testimony with young people. As I wrote in chapters 1 and 2, everything happened very fast. I met my wife in November 1998, in January 1999 we got engaged, on February 11, 1999, we were married, and the same year, on September 15, 1999, I immigrated to Canada. Our first son was born in the same year, on November 14.

I continued to be active in a nearby Catholic Church and also in a growing prayer ministry. In the year 2000, as I was still the part of prayer ministry, we the members used to sit together and pray. God spoke through us, telling us of many things that would happen years later. During these intercessory prayers, one of my spiritual elder got messages from the Lord, and he said, "You need to stay away from all ministries and spend more time in prayer and intercession for others, especially for the Church." I didn't say anything, because I was not very happy about what I was hearing.

I asked him, "Can I still be an active part of prayer ministry."

He said, "No. Again and again, the Lord says he wants you to stay away from all the activities at church and just do intercession."

Initially I was very upset and thought, "Maybe it's not the Lord who is speaking. It's the devil, or perhaps he is jealous of me, because the Lord was doing lots of miracles through me."

Later, I knew it was the Lord who was asking me to stay away from active ministry and go into prayer. So, with much hesitation, I stayed away from active prayer ministry. As it says in Isaiah 55:8, "For my thoughts are not your thoughts, neither are your ways my ways." So the Lord started to work in me mysteriously. I learned to be in complete surrender and submissive to the Lord and to my family. The Lord told me to put the gifts of the Holy Spirit away for a while, and he started to work in me the fruits of the Holy Spirit—love, joy, peace, patience, kindness, goodness, faithfulness, gentleness, and self-control—especially he wanted me to be more patient and control my anger. Sadly, that was a major part of my fight with my wife!

During these times, my faith was tested in many ways. As a growing family, we had our fair struggles adapting to the new place, moving from place to place, changing jobs, facing financial burdens, raising children, enduring sicknesses, and so on.

As I read in the book *Interior Castle* by St. Teresa of Avila, I felt I had been going through the "seven mansions or castles" for the past years. God, in his great mercy, showered me or gifted me the experiences of the "seventh mansion" with all the blessings and gifts of the Holy Spirit, as it says in her book. I had enjoyed heavenly experience through the togetherness of the Father, the Son, and the Holy Spirit. From that great union of the Trinity, the Lord had sent me back to the basics of spirituality; that is, I started to go through the "first mansion," then the "second," then the "third," climbing the spiritual ladder.

Also during this time, I had a chance to read the *Dark Night of the Soul*, by St. John of the Cross. That book helped me a lot during the grieving period of the loss of our twin babies. But above all it was the persistent and enduring faith, which kept me going through the thick and thins of life's hidden surprises.

I just wanted to get a little deeper in the matter of faith. As a Christian,

There are 2 main kinds of faith: *saving faith* and *living faith* (or *walking faith*).

Of *saving faith* it says in Romans 4:1–8; "That we are justified by faith alone. We are not justified by works or by moral behavior, but rather by faith in the God who credits righteousness to the ungodly apart from works." This blessing is not based on religious rituals or on keeping the law, which only serves to condemn us. So, "saving faith is rooted in God's grace, it rests on God's promise, it revels in God's glory, and it relies on God's power."

But apart from this, I would like to go over the "living faith" or the "daily faith" we need as Christians to live our daily life as God wills.

Hebrews 11:6—"And without faith it is impossible to please him, for whoever would draw near to God must believe that he exists and that he rewards those who seek him."

2 Corinthians 5:7—"For we walk by Faith, not by sight."

When Jesus rebuked the disciples in Matthew 8 for having "little faith," Jesus wasn't talking about the saving faith but rather daily living faith (Matthew 8:23–27).

Over the years of walking with the Lord I had noticed that the living faith rises and falls according to the strength of my relationship with the Lord. When I was in constant intimacy with God, the first trial or storm that hit created fear and panic. When we give God the crumbs of our time and attention, our faith and understating in him will weaken.

Fear conquering faith requires an absolute trust in God. It is the kind of faith that has an open heart to whatever God provides for us. It is a faith that is manifested as an utter dependence on the sovereignty of God. When we live by faith, we can trust that God is working out his purpose for us, even when the storm is at its worst.

When I look back, I recall that whenever I had to go through the hardships in life or I feel as if I was stuck in the middle of the stormy sea, with waves raging from every side, the Lord gave me the strength to look upon his face for help rather than look at the raging storm. Sometimes I marvel at how the Lord walks with me through these storms. Even before I had to carry the heavy cross, he gave me a mountaintop experience so that when the time to carry my cross/burden came, I get strength by pondering the experience I had had with him on the higher grounds. This may be through a vision or Word of God or his presence Himself, which increases my faith and leads me through the darkest valley.

I remember an incident that happened in February 2012, when my wife was pregnant with our fifth child. I was at work doing my night shift. It was minus 40 degrees Celsius outside, one of the coldest days of the year in Toronto. Suddenly I got a phone call from home. My wife was screaming at me, saying she couldn't move and was standing and holding to the pillar inside the house. I didn't understand what it was, so I told her to call 911 and go to the hospital. She refused and told me to rush home immediately. My work was only fifteen minutes away, so I rushed home. On my way, I was praying to the Lord, saying nothing should happen to mother and child. When I reached home, I couldn't believe what I saw. My wife was holding onto the pillar very tight, and she was groaning. She had her feet stretched apart as if she were going to give birth. She was hugging the pillar so tightly and wouldn't let it go. She couldn't move a step, and she didn't know if the baby was alive and well. I tried to help her, but she was in excruciating pain. She couldn't even move. Then from there, I called 911. During this time, my other children were in a panic, and the only words that came from my mouth were *Jesus, Jesus, Jesus …*

The ambulance came and took her to the hospital. It was around 2:00 a.m. Because she was pregnant, they took her directly to labor triage. There, my wife and baby were placed under the monitor. My wife got better, but the baby was under close watch. He was very weak. Suddenly my mind went back to few years back, and a terrible thought went through my mind. A chill went through my spine thinking of the similar situation that had happened with our lost twins, Samuel and Nathaniel. I couldn't breathe for few seconds, thinking of it. I stepped out of the triage room and tears started to roll out of my eyes. I started to plead to the Lord and started to say the rosary. I interceded to Mother Mary and all the Saints and also to Samuel and Nathaniel, who are in heaven. I asked them to intercede for their younger brother, to be healthy and grow to full term. Because it was 3:00 a.m., I couldn't call anyone to pray. All I could do was hold the hands of my wife and pray. Tears were rolling out of her eyes. God gave me the strength to say the Divine Mercy Chaplet and also a full decade of rosary. Surprisingly, it was very quiet inside the room. When I was praying, suddenly I saw Samuel and Nathaniel in my spirit. They came down as two tiny angels and went down to my wife's womb, touching and caressing the baby. The baby in the womb stretched himself up and started to move around, playing with his twin brothers. I couldn't believe it, and in amazement, my wife said, "He started to move around in my tummy." With tears in my eyes, I said, "He is playing with his twin brothers, Samuel and Nathaniel, who are visiting from heaven." Then I gave the baby in the womb over to the protection of our Lady of Good Health (Velankanni Mata).

Psalm 23:

The Lord is my Sheppard;
I shall not want
He makes me to lie down in green pastures,
He leads me beside the still waters
He restores my soul
He leads me in the paths of righteousness
For his names sake
Yea, though I walk through the
Valley of the shadow of death,
I will fear no evil,
For you are with me
Your rod and your staff, they comfort me.
You prepare a table before me
In the presence of my enemies.
You anoint my head with oil,
My cup runs over.
Surely goodness and mercy shall
Follow me.
All the days of my life,
And I will dwell in the house of
The Lord forever.

How often do we trust God with our eternal souls yet not our daily needs? When Jesus rebuked the disciples for their lack of faith, he was referring to their failure to trust him in this practical situation. God wants us to trust him not only with our salvation but also with our relationships, our resources, and our future. He wants to see our professed faith in action. He wants us to put our complete trust in him for each detail of our lives.

When we walk close with God and trust him daily, our faith will conquer our fears. When we put our focus on God, fear will fade into the background. At the first sign of fear, our plan of action should be to seek God in prayer.

Many times, we want God to fix our problems instantly. We want the raging waters around us to cease immediately. Yet sometimes in the middle of the crashing waves, God has a word for us. He wants us to deepen our faith and to grow in him before he intervenes. He wants us to follow in faith—no matter how dark our circumstances seem.

Faith that conquers fear depends on absolute trust in God. It is the kind of faith that has an open heart to whatever God provides for us. It is a faith that is manifested as an utter dependence on the sovereignty of God. When we live by faith, and we know that even when the storm is at its worst, we can trust that God in working out his purpose for us.

I would like to relate a couple more instances where God worked miraculously in my life, strengthening my faith.

In 2008, when I was visiting back home for my sister-in-law's wedding, it was a monsoon season (rainy season). One of those days just before the marriage, it rained three days continuously. There was flooding, and traffic was blocked everywhere in the city. One day, my daughter and I were going to my in-laws' house in a car. My father-in-law's chauffeur was driving the car. My older daughter was only five years old at the time. The driver suggested that instead of going through the main road and getting stuck in the traffic, we should take a country road. I agreed, because he knew the roads better than me. Halfway through our journey, there was a small stream of water going across the road, covering two inches of ground. I asked the driver if everything was okay. He assured me everything was fine. Suddenly the water started to rise—one foot, two feet, three feet …

The driver turned around and looked at me in a panic. I looked at his eyes. There was fear stuck there. I told him not to stop but go forward.

Both sides of the road were covered with rice fields. It was a narrow road, and by this time we could not make a U-turn and go in the opposite direction. The water was still rising. I started to pray, and I asked my daughter to pray too. I assured the driver everything was going to be all right and we were only a few feet away from high ground. In fact, I didn't know anything about that road. I told the driver not to turn the engine off but to keep moving forward. My daughter also started to pray. The water now reached the windshield and the side windows. I started to pray loudly and started to rebuke the water and rain to go away. I started to quote from the Bible, describing how God separated the Red Sea and the river Jordan so the Israelites cross through to dry land. My heart started to beat really fast, because I could feel that car was floating on and off the road. I shouted in a loud voice, "Lord, take us to a high ground or save my daughter."

Suddenly the water started to go down, and when I looked outside, we were driving uphill! At that moment I thanked the Lord for saving us. Later, when I spoke with the driver, he said he was not sure we were going to reach home safely. He thanked me for the prayer and courage.

In the year 2015, God blessed us with a beautiful house. The closing date of the house was Friday, April 30. This house was located in a new development, built from the ground up. We were very excited to move into our newly built house, so we got everything packed up and called the movers to come on May 1, 2015, which was a Saturday.

We got all the paperwork done through lawyers beforehand, having learned from our past bitter experience. All the documents had been signed and forwarded to bank for the release of funds, way ahead of scheduled time, around 10:00 a.m. Normally it should take only a couple of hours to get the mortgage approved, because everything was done online nowadays. So we went home happy from lawyer's office. The lawyer said she would give us a call around 12:00 p.m. once the funds had been released.

At home, we were busy packing our stuff, when suddenly I realized it was 1:00 p.m. I called the lawyer's office, and they assured not to worry; it was a Friday, and there would be delays in the mortgage office for approval because of the backup. So we waited patiently until 2:00 p.m.—still no call from the lawyer. I called the lawyer again, because the construction office would close at 5:00 p.m. sharp, and they would not open again until Monday to give us the keys for the house. Moreover, the movers would be coming on Saturday to move our household items, and the new owners would be moving into the house where we are staying right now on Sunday!

The lawyer's secretary answered the phone. She was little bit annoyed with me, because I kept calling them. She told me to call the bank directly and ask what was going on. So I called the bank manager. He said there had been a computer crash down earlier in the day, at the main downtown office, and everything got backed up. He didn't know how long it was going to take. He said, "Hopefully it will be done by 5:00 p.m., or will be moved to Monday next week."

Now I was in a limbo, and I didn't know what to do. Suddenly I felt so helpless. I called the lawyer's office for some consolation, unsure where to turn at that moment. When the lawyer answered the phone, I said, "Thank God it's you and not your secretary!" She asked me if I had received any updates from the bank manager. I told her what the manager had said, and by now it was already 4:00 p.m. Friday. The lawyer then told me that there was a possibility that the builders would charge us $5000 for breaching the contract for not releasing the funds today. I said, "Why is that our problem? It's the bank who is not releasing the funds!"

She said, "I am just pointing out the law to you. It's written in the builder's contract, which you signed." She then said, "It may happen or may not happen. I am just letting you know."

I said, "Thanks" and hung up the phone.

By this time, my wife was very upset, and I didn't know what to tell my children. I just knelt beside Lord's picture and said, "Lord, you lead the way."

We decided to go to our new house, because we still had one hour left, and the bank was working on it. With faith, I told my wife and children the mortgage would be released in one hour, before 5:00 p.m., so we would have to hurry and go get the keys before the builder's office closed. So we set out in faith. My wife was pregnant with our fifth child at the time. My son and my daughter carried the statue of Mother Mary and the rosary. It was around a forty-five-minute drive from our old house to the new house, depending on traffic. That day, traffic was very heavy. Halfway through, it was almost 5:00 p.m. I pulled the car over to the side and called the lawyer for any updates, but she said there had been no answer from the bank, and she didn't think it would happen today. As a last resort, I called the bank manager, but he didn't pick the phone. By this time, it was past 5:00 p.m., and nothing had happened. I was very upset. I told my family there was no point going to the builder's office now, because the funds would not be released today. Moreover, they would have closed the builder's office by 5:00 p.m. I got emotional and said, "Let's go back." Everyone was very upset. I didn't let them know I was upset too. I cheered them up and said, "Let's go around this new area where they are building the houses and compare. That was also a new development area, where I parked the car.

My daughter said, "Dad, you don't know when to joke, as usual."

I just laughed it off and said, "God will have a different plan for us."

I started driving back to our old house. No one said anything. As I was driving back, a Bible verse came to my mind, Mark 9:23—"Nothing is impossible for those who believe." And Matthew 19:26—"With God, everything is possible." I started to recite these verses, and at an intersection, I turned my car around and started to drive back to the new house.

Everybody was surprised, and my wife asked, "What happened?"

I said, "We are getting our new house today."

No one said anything. It was 6:00 p.m., and on the way, I was repeating the Bible verses. We came to our new house, and again I repeated the verses and went to the construction office.

My wife said, "The office will be locked. It's 6:00 p.m. I said, "I will be back with the keys!"

I pushed the latch to the office, and to my surprise, the door opened. The gentleman inside looked at me and said, "I was waiting for you!"

Amazed, I said, "I thought you would have long gone."

He replied, "Normally I am long gone, but today I stayed to do some work!"

I told him what had happened with the whole mortgage situation and said, "My wife and children are in the car, and we have a statue of Mother Mary with us. We want to leave the statue by the fireplace and do a small prayer. Can you give us the keys for the house?" He said he didn't carry the keys. Another gentleman handled all the keys, so I should check the drawer to see if it was there. He said, "He normally locks all the drawers and goes home." With full faith, I walked towards the drawer and pulled it open. To my utter amazement, it opened, and there inside was one set of keys. I took them up. The tag read "Lot 7."

I jumped up and said, "Praise the Lord."

Even he was amazed and said, "Usually he locks it up and goes, but today it's your day!"

The righteous will live by faith.
—Habakkuk 2:4

CHAPTER 9

My Journey to Purgatory

2 Maccabees 12: 43-45, 46

"But if he was looking to the splendid reward that is laid up for those who fall asleep in godliness, it was a holy and pious thought. Therefore, he made atonement for the dead, so that they might be delivered from their sin."

So, it is a holy and beneficial thought to pray on behalf of those who have passed away, so that they may be released from sins.

According to the Catechism of the Catholic Church (CCC), purgatory is a "final purification which means "all who die in God's grace and friendship, but still imperfectly purified, so that they might achieve the holiness necessary to enter the joy of heaven (CCC1030).

The souls in purgatory are called "Holy Souls", they have died in God's grace and they will attain heaven and to the Glorious Presence of God after their purification is complete. During their life time these souls have been baptised, and received other sacraments, but later fell into sin or lost their faith or didn't get sacrament of reconciliation at their final journey (death).

1 Cor 3:15; "If the work is burned up, the builder will suffer loss; the builder will be saved, but only as through fire."

So many Catholics or Christians die with attachments to sin that must be got rid of before they can be united with Lord in a perfect union of love through all eternity. Purgatory is a place removing this attachment to sin so that souls can love God alone through the painful process and prayers of others on earth and heaven. So, it's a place of purification for the soul, for good. And not a torment, to eternal punishment.

Therefore, a temporary period of purging is necessary to enjoy the presence and glory of God that we were made for, whether we willingly undertake that purging while here on Earth, through our daily crosses given to us by the Lord, or whether after death, in purgatory.

In the year 2016 my mom was visiting us here in Canada. When I met her at the airport, I saw that she was still grieving over the untimely death of her brother. I didn't have words to console her. One evening we sat down for a family prayer. During the prayer, I accidently reminded her that, how she had lost 2 of her brothers suddenly to death. Then I saw tears rolling down her cheeks. I felt bad for her. I didn't say anything more, but in my heart, I started to grieve and asked Lord, "where are they now, Lord? Are they in heaven or hell or the place called purgatory," because I love them too and I know one of my uncle didn't have final confession/ reconciliation or the sacrament of the 'anointing of the sick', because of the untimely death.

While I was still grieving and praying, suddenly Lord took me in spirit to a place. From high above it looked very dark and gloomy. But when I got closer, I saw a very dim light. In that dim light I saw there were thousands of people buried in the ground – some till their neck, some till their chest, some till their waist, some till their knee and some just their feet covered. They looked like they were glued to the ground, and could not come out of it. Even they could not move a bit. There was no presence of God there, it was so empty and void.

These people/souls were crying and asking for help. Suddenly, from a distance I saw my uncles face and I recognized him. But I couldn't talk to him. As I was watching him from distance, I saw 2 small angels coming down from heaven towards my uncle. I immediately recognized them. They are my twin babies Samuel and Nathaniel who died within few hours, after they were born, few years back. When I saw them I couldn't hold myself up. I wanted to get closer to them. Then I saw them giving something to my uncle to drink. And he gobbled down the throat and he thanked them for it. It looked like water. When I got closer, Samuel and Nathaniel saw me and came towards me exited and hugged me. I asked them what did they give the uncle. They said, "its to quench the thirst of

51

the spirit. It's the prayers from saints in heaven, which will help them to console and comfort them while they are here in Purgatory.

I asked Samuel and Nathaniel again, "but why are they thirsty". They said, "here, there is no presence of God and they are constantly thirsting for his presence and mercy. And also, there is an absence of the grace of God and these souls can't pray for themselves but depend on the prayers and supplications of their immediate family and relatives on Earth and the saints in Heaven, which will help them to come out of this place".

I was sad in my heart. They said, "don't worry, go back to your mom and ask her to pray for him and his brother. Suddenly I opened my eyes and told my mom what I saw, and asked her to pray for her brothers. When she heard that, she started to cry loudly and started to pray for them and we also started to pray for our uncle. Then again, I was amazed at what I saw; the prayers my mom prayed 'weeping', became a fountain of water in that brim light and it was flooding over his head and spreading over the area he was buried and soaking the dry ground around him and he was comforted greatly. I greatly rejoiced seeing that, and when I looked around I saw others receiving prayers from their families and the souls were greatly overjoyed and consoled. Also, I saw angles coming down from heaven and helping these souls.

When I looked up, I saw a step up or a platform. It was a huge platform. When I approached closer I saw lots of people/souls lying down with closed eyes, some opened their eyes and looked up and with great joy and content they went back to sleep again. I asked an angel, "who are they." Then the angel replied, "they are the souls which came out of purgatory, but still waiting for God's call. So, they could be taken up to heaven. When I came closer, I saw my other uncle at peace sleeping and waiting to go up to heaven.

I opened my eyes again and told what I saw in spirit and my mom found some consolation in those words.

And I recited these words from Apostles Creed: "He will come again to judge the living and the dead. I believe in the Holy Spirit, Holy Catholic Church, Communion of Saints and Life Everlasting.

Amen

Printed in the United States
by Bookmasters

Printed in the United States
By Bookmasters